Developing Your Real Estate Career by The Numbers

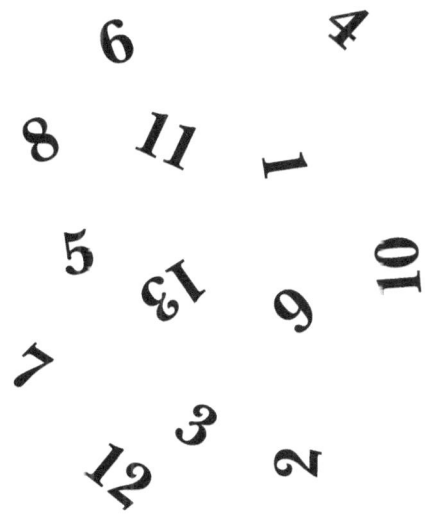

M. CORDELL

authorHOUSE™

1663 LIBERTY DRIVE, SUITE 200
BLOOMINGTON, INDIANA 47403
(800) 839-8640
WWW.AUTHORHOUSE.COM

First published by AuthorHouse 11/10/05

ISBN: 1-4208-9516-8(sc)

Publisher: Author House
Editor: Allyson Newbold (author of The Treasure of All Time)

Library of Congress Control Number: 2005909892

Printed in the United States of America
Bloomington, Indiana

This book is printed on acid-free paper.

Disclosures:

The contents of this
guide are ideas and
concepts of the
Author
and intentions of
these concepts are
to be used only as
tools to help
with the readers'
goals.

Preface

"Developing your Career by the Numbers" book is a tool for success, not a guarantee of success. Along with tools and direction, a Realtor needs to be a self motivated individual.

I became a part of the Real Estate arena 15 years ago. When I received my license and was assigned my desk, I was totally lost and confused. I asked myself, "what have I done"? But I was self motivated, eager to learn, understood marketing, and had been self employed prior to becoming a Realtor.

This, with hits and misses, I found proven directions to take to develop my career as a Real Estate professional. Since starting my own company, I found the need to share these concepts with my own agents, thus helping them be more comfortable, more knowledgeable, more motivated, and eager to be successful.

Some people may disagree with my ideas and concepts, and I fully understand. You the reader, especially if you are a new agent, need to take time and devour these ideas and take them forward in your life. Everything here is not for everyone, but if only a few concepts help you, I will be pleased.

Thank you
And Stay Motivated!

Contents

Chapter 16.
6 Steps to Understanding the 1031

Chapter 1.
7 Steps to
Getting Started

Your first day at the
office - What a gut
achy feeling! Now
what? You said hello
to everyone, okay
cool - ahh, now
where is my desk?

Meet with your new Broker or sales manager and complete all necessary paperwork.

Set up your voice mail. Do your layout for business cards and your profile information for the company website. Order your name tag, sign riders, and car signs.

Read Developing your Real Estate Career by the Numbers.

Get familiar with the company listings. Where do they keep the book?

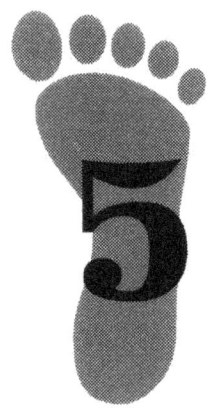

Check out the entire office, conference room, tax maps, office procedures, and who does what

Start a day timer - log everything down.

Items you need - computer, digital camera, day timer, folders, pads, business cards, pen/pencils, exposure log, and a big smile

Chapter 2.
8 Steps to
Developing
Contacts

Real Estate is just like any business, you need customers, or a better term - contacts. How to get these contacts is very simple, but you need patience and motivation to build your contact list. It takes work, time, and being consistent. Contacts = sales. Sales = $ in your pocket.

First thing you do is send a letter to everyone you know; family, friends, doctors, dentist, auto repairman, builder, school teacher, neighbors, hair dresser, fitness director, church, etc..., State that you need their help getting started.

Use your car signs, pass out business cards, promote your own website, distribute flyers with photo, and sign up with the Chamber of Commerce. Be involved with the community in some way. Contact old school mates and always, always be positive and excited about your new career.

Hold open houses - Chapter 3

Floor duty/opportunity time - Chapter 4

Self marketing - Chapter 9

 FSBO'S
Chapter 5

 Farming -
Chapter 6

 Me by the
numbers
Chapter 7

Chapter 3.
14 Steps for
an Excellent
Open House

Open houses: the good, the bad, and the ugly. Yes, everyone has an opinion. I am a firm believer in open houses. I can think of no better way to meet and talk to people than at open houses. Yes you hear stories of how no one shows up, it rained all day, it was boring, or the neighbor just wanted to snoop around. The list could go on. Then there are the days the buyers show up. It's a good feeling when you have a completed contract in your hand.

Open houses let you build, develop and acquire skills for the future. The low volume of traffic lets you develop style and confidence, as well as meet and understand buyers needs and wants. This may not be the home you sell - it may only be the opportunity to sell another home.

So do open houses, have fun, experiment with listening skills. It works!

Check your
schedule - know
when and where
you have to be. Let
the seller know
you are coming.

Be on time, be
ready, be
prepared. Signs?
Balloons?
Camera?
Business cards?
Profile sheet?
Sign in sheet?
Pens? Paper?

Turn on all
the lights.

Turn on ceiling fans.

Open the blinds, curtains - let light in.

Make sure bathrooms are stocked with toilet paper, paper towels, and hand soap.

Keep on hand
paper plates,
napkins,
forks, cups,
and snacks.

Bring a radio,
your laptop,
cell phone, a
folding chair
if the house is
new, vacant, or
unfurnished.

Lay out your
guests sheets,
profile sheets,
and property
disclosures.
Hand out
lender
packets with
business cards.

Put signs and balloons out.

Relax, be positive, and get in the mood to sell.

When someone arrives get up and greet them, smile, and tell them to please take a look around. Don't be pushy, be calm and ask questions; Does this fit your needs? Location good? Like this style of home? Would you like to see something else?

Follow up at the end of the day by sending out Thank You cards. Just say thank you for stopping by.

Put attendees in your data base.

*Having something to
eat or drink is always
nice to have, especially
if children come in
with the parents. Offer
cookies, candy, or a cold
soda.

*Offer gift certificates
- Thanks for coming -
Little things help!

Chapter 4.
6 Steps to An Excellent Office Opportunity Time

Most Real Estate Companies offer what is now known as opportunity time, or also known as non-paid floor duty, and negatively known as receptionist duty. No matter what the name or time slot, this can be turned into what I call a chance to sell. Yes, you will have to answer the phones. Yes, you will have to set appointments for other agents. Yes, you will have to set out keys for others. Yes, you will have to give directions and so forth.

Then it's the call that says, "Can you help me buy a home?" I don't have a realtor." Yes I can!

Contacts = Sales
Sales = $ in your pocket

Be on time, be prepared. Setup listing books, know where keys are, layout map so you can explain directions.

Review listing book - find out if any changes need to be made.

Review showing instructions.

Have a pad and pencil ready.

While waiting on calls, update your data base, work on new weekly goals, go on-line and review other companies listings.

Have a good
attitude - You
represent the
company and
enthusiasm is
contagious.

Attitude Is
Everything.

Chapter 5.
8 Steps to working with
FSBO'S

FSBO or For Sale by Owner is an opportunity to convert a potential seller to trust and build confidence in a Realtor.

Always have a plan. With FSBO's, they honestly feel they can do a better job at selling their house. Also, most have had (in my experience) a bad experience with a Realtor. So I designed the enclosed flyer to mail to them. I never call a FSBO, I'd rather mail an nice card with my flyer and business card. This lets them know who I am and what my intentions are.

I simply state that
if I have a potential
buyer, would you
allow me to show
your home and pay
me my commission?
Then I show it. I
try to have an open
house in the
community, so I can
tell others it's
available for
showing. Let the
seller know you are
a working Realtor.

When working
your farm area,
be alert to
FSBO's. They
have already
seen your name
and marketing
materials.

When the sign
goes up, send
the enclosed
flyer along
with your
business card.

Alert them
that you
know their
home is for
sales.

Stop by and ask if you can preview their home. Talk to them. Ask why they are not using a licensed Realtor?

Show interest, be understanding, be upbeat, and be available for help.

Try to show the property with a one time showing agreement.

Build trust with the seller.

Put information into your data base under "FSBO's for sale."

Chapter 6.
6 Steps to Farming a Community

Farming. I have seen so many Realtors give up and quit before the fruits of their work is known. Farming is a great way to build name recognition. It's easy, not very expensive and a huge opportunity to make contacts. Contacts = sales   Sales = $ in your pocket.

Locate a community that you know, live in, or feel good about.

Research the community. How old is it? Who were the builders? How many homes? Schools? Taxes? HOA fees? Amenities? What is positive?

Plan for the long haul. Farming is not easy. Just ask a real farmer.

 Design an intro letter, flyer, and post card. (See Samples)

 Plan mail times - review costs.

 Once you start - Don't Stop!

A good farm should
be 250 to 500 homes.
Set up a separate
data base for this
and track all
mailings, calls,
FSBO's, and try to get
your listings there.
Have open houses, let
people know you are serious.

Chapter 7.
10 Steps to
Realize Me

What is this all about?
10 steps of me? Well, if
you are going to be a
professional Realtor,
you have to understand
yourself before you
can understand others.

It's the Self Image by
the Numbers

Attitude

Self
confidence

Good listener

Good eye contact

Expression (smiles)

Caring / understanding

On Time

Being prepared

Appearance

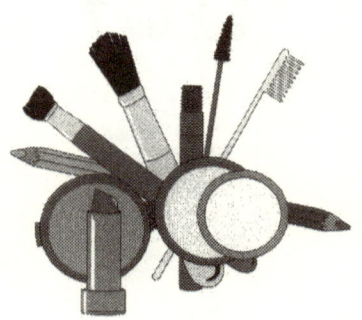

Excitement

How I Am
How I Look
How I Talk
How I Care
This is
Me!!

Chapter 8.
9 Steps to
Do at the
Office
Each Day

Even if you don't plan to work out of the main office or sit at your desk for the day, go to the office and check in. Say hello to the staff. Let them know that you are in the building working and let them know you are excited! Every day you should do these 9 steps.

 Check your mailbox.

 Check your company e-mail.

 Check your voice mail.

Check
your desk
for memos
or notes.

Check the
bulletin
board.

Check
phone
logs - who
called in
for you?

Check with
floor duty
agent - let
them know
your plans.

Check with
the Broker or
Sales
Manager, let
them know
you are in.

Check
listing book -
Anything
new?
Anything
sold?

Making an appearance
if for only a few minutes
or an hour will go a long
way with the staff and
management.

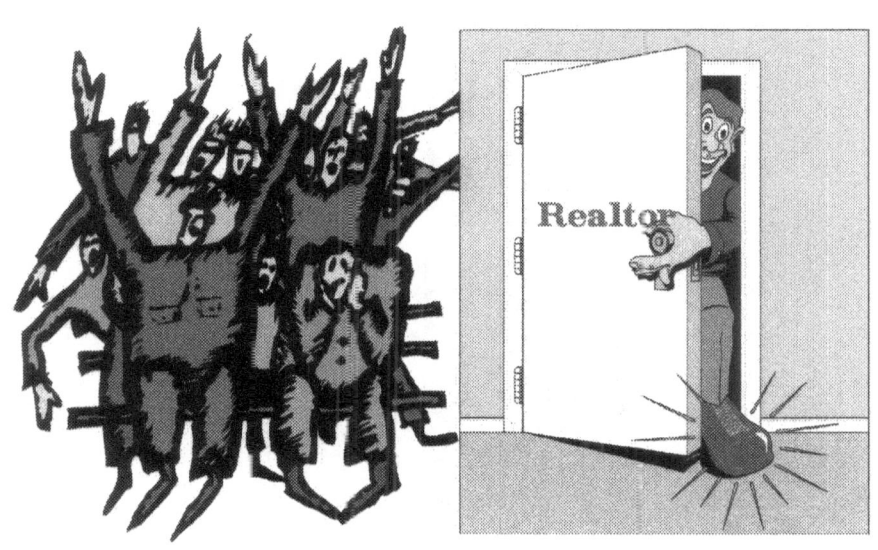

Chapter 9.
6 Steps to Building New Business

As in any business, you need to continuously market, advertise, make contacts, and focus on what you are doing and why.

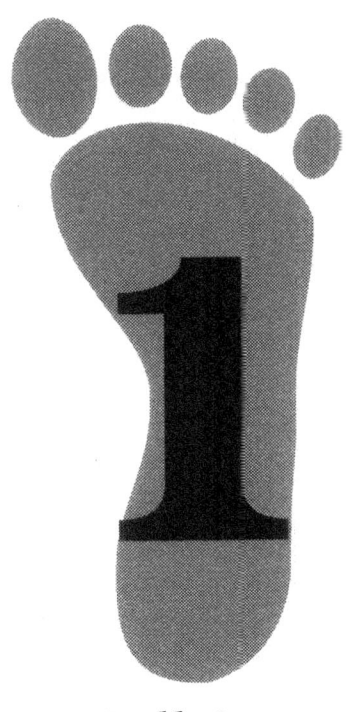

Schedule telephone time.

> Call 6 people everyday that you know or have met.

> Call 6 people everyday that you have never met.

> Call 6 people you have sold to.

Keep in touch with prospects.

> Call 6 of them - get an update.

> Write 6 of them a letter.

> Visit 6 of them - say hello.

3 Networking "Very Key"

> Go to 6 luncheons this month

> Go to 6 meetings - clubs, classes, the chamber, county meetings.

> Go to 6 grand openings, new businesses, new communities, new recreational facilities.

4 Stay focused - don't let time eat away your day. Plan 6 hours of Real Estate time.

Real Estate time

6 hours

 # Your
Data
Bases.

> Review the past 6 months entries.

>Delete anyone that refuses to respond.

> Review the past 6 days: Did I do a good job? Did I send out Thank You Cards?

Marketing - It's all about you.

6 Steps to Remember

1. Market your company.
2. Market your name.
3. Market your location.
4. Market your listings.
5. Market your friends.
6. Market your excitement.

Chapter 10.
4 Steps to
Getting
Listings

If you don't have listings, you can't sell them. If you rely on the listings of others, you will not be as successful.

 The one question almost every new Realtor will ask....Where do leads or contacts come from?

Well, here is a rough idea. It's not written in stone, but very clear and it's easy to validate.

Company Referrals		**20%**
Walk in Traffic		**5%**
Signage	ABC Realty	**15%**
Open Houses		**6%**
Advertising	Sell	**9%**
		55%

Individual contacts

33%

Sale and listing contacts

12%

45%

So lets talk this out. If you do office opportunity time, hold open houses, make an appearance in the office, and know company product, you have an opportunity to make contacts and Contact = Sales and Sales = $ in your pocket.

Now 45% of all sales and/or listings come from you! Your contacts, your sales, your listings, and your marketing.

Establish
your own
personal referral
tree. Why
do that?
Read on.

Golf

Cars

Church

Handyman

Restaurant

Tanning

Fishing

Appliances

When people are in
need, refer them to a
specific person.
Build a rapport. Let
them know you are
sending someone to
them.   Put the
information in your
data base, these
people will
remember you and
refer a buyer or
seller back to you.

Set up a contact system.

Use Act data base or similar product

Use the Address book on your computer

Use 3X5 cards

Use a ledger book

Just use
something -
Put name,
address,
telephone,
dates, details,
and personal
comments.

My
Contacts.....

Visibility

Leave business cards everywhere, write letters, stop and say hello. Use company free-bees, sticky pads, letter head, pens, etc... Anything that's free you can put your name on. Keep in touch. Look sharp, be energetic, smile, keep your car clean and neat. Do open houses - a great way to find sellers.

4 Farming

Do your farm area,
your neighborhood.
Get out meet and
greet, let them
know who and
what you are and
do.

Know your farm
area. Learn more
about it. Number
of homes, HOA
fees, pools,
restaurants,
prices, and
neighbors. Set up
maps, plats, HOA
rules, taxes, and
insurance. Set up
directions to the
hospital, schools,
shopping, and
recreation.

Don't be
ashamed of
what you do,
let them know.
Be proud, be
honest, be
professional.
That is what a
Realtor is.

Chapter 11.
4 Steps toward success

Successful people
are organized
people.

Plan your day - Get ready and be ready.

> Have at hand a yellow pad and pen

>Calculator

>Day timer

>Block out your day

Be prepared

> Have business cards

>To do list

>Name tags

>Schedule plenty of time

Be Ready

> Have a sign in the car

> Listing packets

> Camera

> Tape measure

> Flash light

> Procedure book

Have a purpose.

Don't go just
running
about - have a
purpose for
your day.

Chapter 12.
4 Steps in Getting Great Inexpensive Exposure

These steps are just a few that you can use to get your name out there. It's all about you! There are many inexpensive ways to get the job done.

Place mats

For as little as $200 - $300 you can have your picture numbers, e-mail, and web site in front of 15,000 breakfast eaters! Simple and it works!

ABC Realty

John Doe 236-5432

Card
Racks

Easy to do, just supply
the business cards and
there are in 1, 2, 3,
4, 5, up to 25
Restaurants or other
businesses. Again,
inexpensive advertising
and name exposure.

Gift Baskets

This is a great idea for a Just Listed or Just Sold - Thank you for the referral, Happy Birthday, Welcome Home and so on. A small basket with candy, coffee, tea, bread sticks, and so forth, with your business card and a personal statement means a lot. People remember these things and that's the goal.

Business Cards

Leave them everywhere - car wash, repair shops, grocery stores, toy stores, etc... It's non threatening to take a card home. It's simple and free advertising.

Business card

Chapter 13.
8 Steps in managing your listings

It always amazes me when a Realtor gets a listing, puts it in the MLS and then...nothing. It's forgotten and left alone. It's difficult to get that listing and in order to profit from it, you need to manage it. Get it sold. Sales = $ in your pocket.

Once you get the listing in the MLS, send out flyers in that neighborhood.

Start open houses. Do them daily if you need to.

Post "for sale" sign, put out balloons, put an inexpensive classified ad in the local papers.

Search your
data base,
review past
buyers. Does
this fit?

Keep seller
informed of
what, where,
and how you
are doing. Send
an update letter
every 30 days.

Take pictures,
lots of them. Get
them on the
company web
site along with
your personal
web site.

Make up a nice profile sheet; something simple and easy to read. Highlight key areas. Fax this to all Real Estate Companies in your area.

Be proud of your listing regardless of the sell price. Be excited and energized. Let your office, seller and possible buyers see your enthusiasm.

Chapter 14.
4 Steps to Setting Real Goals

I like sitting down with agents, especially new agents, when it's time for the upcoming new year's goal setting. I find it exciting! Too many new agents, and even agents with several years experience, fail to set goals and follow through. It's important to know where you are, where you want to go, and how you're going to get there.

Forget about being a million dollar producer... you'll be broke. $1,000,000 in sales divided by 2 agencies, divided by your own company, equals $15,000 less expenses for the year. This is estimated at about $500 per month or $6,000 less self employment taxes of 15% at $1350 = $7650. That's not being successful.

Sit down with a pad and pencil. Look back over the last year and put down your results. How many listings did I have? How many sales did I have? What was my monthly expenses? Find out how many sells and divide that into dollars. What was my average $ value per transaction? Summarize your information.

Look at your numbers and lets project the next 12 months. What's the market like? Interest rates? Mood of the economy? Put down the number of transactions you feel you can complete. Add referrals, add selling bonuses to get your total.

Now you have your goals. Review last year's open houses, ads, flyers, and faxes. Where was I weak? Where can I improve? What didn't I do? If you kept your records, you can solve this quickly. Look at where you got the best results.

Goals are just goals. They need commitment. It takes courage, inner strength and self motivation to get results. Make your commitment. Review your goals daily. Try new things. Test the waters. Be Bold!

Chapter 15.
10 Steps of
Do's and
Don'ts

Don't   Do

Don't get caught up in the million dollar theme.

Don't focus on the "Big Hit" or "once in a life time" sale.

Don't get caught up in the commission struggle, be flexible, be open. Make the transaction profitable.

Don't look at your financial situation transaction by transaction.

Don't get caught up into heavy expenses and long learning curves.

Heavy expenses

Big Deal

Commission

Do Focus on every opportunity, large and small.

Do Be an opportunist, honest, and a hard worker.

Do Look at being the best you can be. Do the job right, do it because you love it.

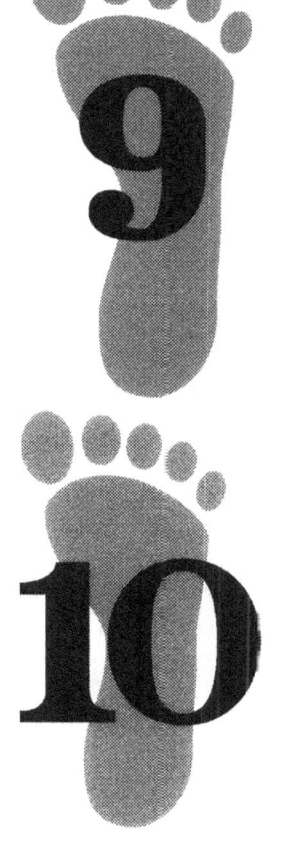

9

Do Let people learn about you, know you, and understand that you are a professional Realtor.

10

Do Learn new technology

Chapter 16.
6 Steps to Understanding the 1031 Exchange

Section 1031 of the Internal Revenue Code provides for nonrecognition treatment of the gain or loss arising from the exchange of property of a like kind. It has been in the Internal Revenue Code since 1924, and has remained substantially unchanged since that time.

Section 1031 is available for all types of operating assets, and over the decades, businesses have exchanged everything from railroad cars to restaurant equipment under Section 1031. One type of business property eligible for Section 1031, is real estate.

If you are considering structuring a real estate transaction as a like-kind exchange, the very first thing you should do is analyze the income tax consequences of structuring the deal as a like-kind exchange, versus the income tax consequences of not structuring the deal as a like-kind exchange.

Section 1031 does not eliminate the income tax on appreciated property; it merely defers the tax. Nonetheless, the ability to defer income tax on the appreciation in real estate under Section 1031 can be a powerful financial tool.

The Mechanics of Section 1031

Whether an interest in real estate is eligible for like-kind treatment depends upon the use of the real estate. Only two types of real estate qualify for nonrecognition treatment under Section 1031: property used in a trade or business, and property held for investment.

Both properties, the property given up and the property received, must either be used in a trade or business, or as an investment. Section 1031 does not apply to real estate which would be considered inventory or personal use property.

Section 1031 looks to
the use of the asset
at the time of
exchange in order to
determine it's
character for tax
purposes. If at the
time of the exchange
the taxpayer uses the
old property in a
trade or business, or
holds it for
investment, and if,
immediately after the
exchange, the
taxpayer uses the
replacement property
in a trade or business, or
holds it
for investment, both
parties will be
eligible for Section
1031.

If, on the other hand, either property is personal use property or inventory in the hands of the taxpayer at the time of the exchange, the transaction is ineligible for Section 1031.

WE'RE IN THIS TOGETHER!

Although the rules governing the use of the properties are strict, the regulations permit a great deal of flexibility regarding the types of real estate which can be exchanged. Here are a few examples of the types of real estate interests which can be exchanged under Section 1031.

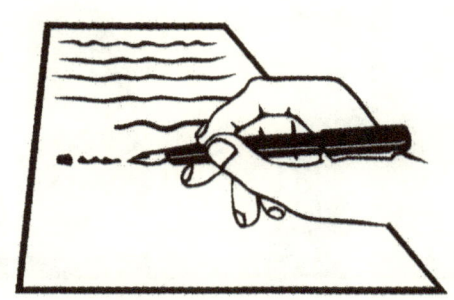

> raw land for a building

> a house for an office building

> farm land for urban real estate

> several parcels for one parcel

> one parcel for several parcels

> investment property for property to be used in trade or business

> an interest as a joint tenant or tenant in common for an interest as a sole owner

> any combination of the above examples

As long as both properties, the property given up and the property received, are used in a trade or business, or held for investment, the properties will qualify for Section 1031.

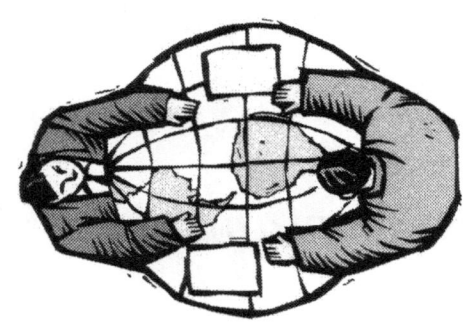

Common Methods of Exchanges & the Safe Harbor Regulation

Direct Swaps - The simplest form of exchange is a direct swap, in which you simply deliver a deed to the old property in exchange for a deed to the replacement property.

Three-Cornered Exchanges - Often the sale of the old property can be characterized as a like-kind exchange, even though the seller of the new property does not want to swap it for the old property. For example, suppose you hold a parcel of appreciated raw land. You find a townhouse which is for sale for a fantastically low price, but you do not have funds sufficient to purchase it.

The owner of the house wants cash and is not interested in owning your land. If you can locate a buyer who wants to pay cash for your land, the seller of the townhouse can swap the townhouse for your land, and sell the land to your buyer. This structure is known as a "three cornered exchange", or a "deferred like-kind exchange".

Another type of three-cornered exchange is to have the buyer purchase the townhouse, and in turn swap it with you in exchange for the land. This can often all be done at one settlement table, and usually involves little more than having the taxpayer's seller or buyer agreeing to serve as the middleman.

Use of an Escrow Agent in Three-Cornered Exchanges - If your seller is unwilling to cooperate in a like-kind exchange, if you are having problems, or if you are doing a multi-parcel exchange with multiple parties, you can use an escrow agent to structure a like-kind exchange.

Use of an Escrow Agent when You Have No Replacement Property - If you have not located replacement property at the time of settlement, you could convey the real estate to an escrow agent and have the escrow agent sell it for cash. If you can identify replacement property within forty-five days, the escrow agent can purchase the replacement property, and swap it with you for your old real estate.

Use of an Escrow Agent to Exchange Multiple Parcels - Suppose you have several parcels of appreciated real estate which you want to swap for one large parcel of real estate, but the owner of the large parcel wants cash. Or suppose you own a large parcel of appreciated real estate and wish to exchange it for several smaller parcels owned by different people. In both cases you can use an escrow agent to take title to your real estate, sell it for cash, purchase the new real estate, and swap it in exchange for the old real estate.

The solution is to swap the old property for the replacement property. After a year or two, you can refinance the new property by borrowing $2,000,000 against the property, and securing the loan with a mortgage. As a result, you will own the replacement property, and you will have $2,000,000 in cash, free of income tax.

The Safe Harbor
Regulations -
These regulations
define several
safe harbors,
within which you
can operate with
confidence that
the IRS with not
challenge the
transaction.

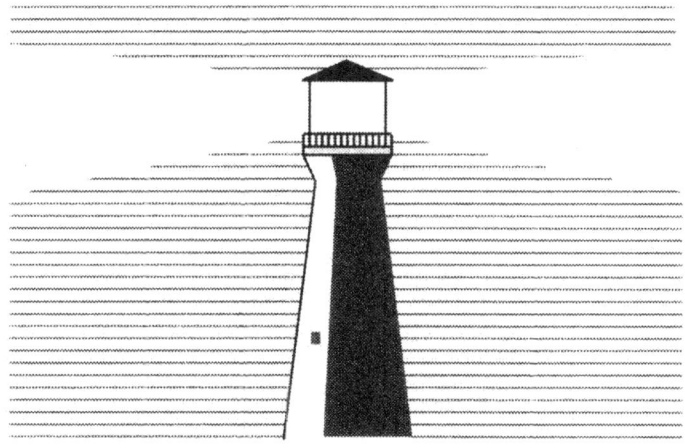

Safe Harbor No. 1: Mortgage or Letter of Credit

Under the first safe harbor, the taxpayer can have the buyer of the old property purchase the replacement property, and convey it to the taxpayer. The obligation of the purchaser of the old property to transfer the replacement property is permitted to be secured by a mortgage. It can also be secured by a stand-by letter of credit except upon failure of the purchaser to transfer like-kind replacement property.

Safe Harbor No. 2: Cash Held in Escrow

Under the second safe harbor, the obligation of the buyer to transfer the replacement property is permitted to be secured by cash held in an escrow account.

Safe Harbor No. 3: A Qualified Intermediary

Under the third safe harbor, the seller can utilize a "qualified intermediary" to transact the deferred exchange. A "qualified intermediary" is a person who is not related to the taxpayer (a family member, attorney of the taxpayer, or a business associate), and who, for a fee if he wishes, acts to facilitate the exchange by entering into an agreement for the exchange of properties.

The agreement must state that the intermediary will acquire the old property, accept the proceeds, acquire the replacement property with the proceeds and transfer the replacement property to the seller.

Direct Deeds -
Under the
third safe
harbor, and
under Revenue
Ruling 90-34,
the IRS now
permits direct
deeds.

Interest or Growth Factor - The seller can even specify that the seller is to receive the interest on the sales price until the replacement property is acquired. The seller can also specify a growth factor for the proceeds, which would require the buyer to purchase a higher - priced replacement property. If the seller receives the interest, the interest will be taxable to the seller, but it will not disqualify the transaction from like-kind treatment.

Reverse Exchanges - On September 15, 2000, the IRS issued Revenue Procedure 2000-37, which now provides a safe harbor for a reverse like-kind exchange. In a reverse like-kind exchange, the taxpayer acquires the replacement property before he disposes of his old property, usually by means of a bridge loan.

The safe harbor requires the execution of a Qualified Exchange Accommodation Agreement, by an Exchange Accommodation Titleholder. Rev. Proc. 2000-37 sets forth other requirements for the safe harbor as well. You can obtain a copy of Rev. Proc. 2000-37 at www.irs.gov

The Treatment of Cash & Mortgages

The Treatment of Boot - The receipt of boot 9 any non like-kind property, which includes cash) by the taxpayer will not make the transaction ineligible for Section 1031 treatment.

However, any boot received by the taxpayer will be taxable to the extent of the gain the taxpayer has realized. You can swap your real estate partly for real estate and partly for cash. However, you will have to recognize gain on the exchange to the extent of the cash that you receive.

The Treatment of Mortgages - Under the Internal Revenue Code, relief of indebtedness is considered income. Under Section 1031, if you swap property with a mortgage in exchange for property which is mortgage - free, the principal amount of the mortgage on the old property will be considered income to you. However, Section 1031 has special rules which permit the netting of mortgages. If you trade mortgaged property in exchange for new mortgage equals or exceeds the principal amount of your old mortgage, and you will not have to recognize income on the exchange.

Use of the Mortgages to Avoid Recognition of Gain - The Tax Court has approved the liberal use of mortgages to facilitate like-kind exchanges. The ability to utilize mortgages provides great flexibility in structuring like-kind exchanges, even enabling the taxpayer to pull cash out of the real estate tax-free.

Time Limits
& Basis
Adjustments

Time Restrictions upon Like-Kind Exchanges - The settlement date on the old property is the trigger date for two time restrictions upon a like-kind exchange. The new property must be identified within 45 days after the settlement date for the transfer of the old property. In addition, settlement on the new property must occur within 180 days after settlement on the old property.

Basis Adjustments under Section 1031 - Section 1031 does not eliminate the income tax on the appreciation of real estate. It is simply a method to defer the tax, even though the taxpayer is changing the form of this investment. Section 1031 defers the tax by requiring the owner to transfer to the new property the same basis he had in the old property. In tax parlance, this is known as a carryover basis. The carryover basis is increased by any cash which the taxpayer contributes to the purchase of the new property.

If you are selling appreciated investment or business real estate, and you plan to use the proceeds to purchase new real estate, you may wish to structure the transaction as a like-kind exchange under Section 1031. Section 1031 will allow you to defer the tax on the appreciation of the old real estate. The regulations allow a great deal of flexibility in structuring like-kind exchanges, so that Section 1031 deferral is available in a variety of circumstances.

Closing

As Realtors we are given the opportunity to help a vast number of people in our career life, simply by taking a few hours of courses, getting a license and joining our local MLS board.

We have the
power to work
with people that
invest from
thousands of
dollars to
millions of
dollars. They look
to us as
guardians, the
professionals, for
leadership and
trustworthiness.

We need to be
professionals,
trustworthy,
honest, and
devoted to our
career.

I believe that
all Realtors
need to continue
with education,
training, and
self improvement. It's
such a small
expense for the
responsibility
we carry.

Sample Flyers

Thank You Card

*Blank inside to write a message

Farming Postcard

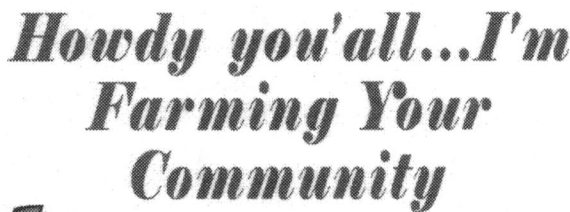

Postcard

ABC Realty

Business Growing? Need to Expand? Ready to Retire? Looking for a New Venture?

At ABC Realty we work with commercial buyers and sellers to find a plan that works best for them. Leasing, selling and/or building, we want to be your Real Estate Guide.

222.123.2BUY   *www.abcrealty.com*

Market Analysis

Competitive Market Analysis

If you are interested in a Competitive Market Analysis of your property simply complete and return this certificate - or call me today! This information is valuable for reviewing insurance, estate planning, financing, buying, selling, or investing.

Name_____
Address_____
City_____State/Zip_____
Daytime Phone___
Evening Phone_____
Best Time to Call_____

ABC Realty

222.123.2BUY   *www.abcrealty.com*

Notepad With Logo

ABC Realty

Phone: 222.123.2BUY

55 Sell St. Smithville, SC 29555
www.abcrealty.com

Buying is as easy as 1-2-3

Step #1
Decide what type of neighborhood you would feel comfortable living in.
Step #2
What type of home do you need?
Step #3
Now to crunch the numbers...

222.123.2BUY
www.abcrealty.com
and make your purchase!

*Inside brochure would list all three steps throughout three pages and add more detail

About The Author

Major Cordell has been in the Real Estate Business for 15 years covering all facets of the industry including Land Development, Commercial, Residential and Land Sales.

Major Cordell also has been in the Home Building Business for 3 years doing investment spec homes with small investors.

Cordell Realty opened in 2003 and has grown from 1 agent to 20 agents. The company is currently seeking Satellite offices to expand the area of operation.

Major has always been one to encourage his agents to learn new things, promote new ideas, keep up with current laws and maintain job knowledge. He has an on-going training program, held on a monthly basis, which is fully funded by his Company.

Being in love with what you do makes you the Realtor you need to be.

www.ingramcontent.com/pod-product-compliance
Lightning Source LLC
Chambersburg PA
CBHW021952170526
45157CB00003B/956